WORLD WAR TWO

Sue Graves

Rising Stars UK Ltd.
22 Grafton Street, London W1S 4EX
www.risingstars-uk.com

NASEN House, 4/5 Amber Business Village, Amber Close, Amington, Tamworth, Staffordshire B77 4RP

Every effort has been made to trace copyright holders and obtain their permission for the use of copyright materials. The publisher will gladly receive information enabling them to rectify any error or omission in subsequent editions.

All facts are correct at time of going to press.

Published 2008

Series Consultant: Lorraine Petersen
Cover design: Neil Straker Creative
Cover photograph: Alamy
Design: Clive Sutherland
Editorial: Frances Ridley
Illustrations: Bill Greenhead for Illustration Ltd
Photographs: AKG Images: 26, 36
Alamy: 23, 34, 35, 38-39, 40, 41, 44, 45, 47
The Art Archive: 6, 7, 12, 14, 24, 35, 42, 46
Getty Images: 6, 7, 8, 13, 30
Kobal Collection: 7, 4, 7, 20
PA Photos: 46

British Library Cataloguing in Publication Data.
A CIP record for this book is available from the British Library.

ISBN: 978-1-84680-449-6

Printed by: Craftprint International Ltd, Singapore

Contents

WORLD WAR TWO: THE BIG PICTURE

World War Two was a terrible war. It began in Europe and then spread across many parts of the world. It lasted from 1939 to 1945. In six short years more than 55 million people died.

Find the answers to these questions.

1. What were dogfights?
2. How were pencils used to kill people?
3. Who used a folding motorbike?

ZOOMING IN ...

We will fight them on the beaches.

Pilots battle it out.

Resistance groups fight back.

Hitler invades Poland ... it's war!

Thousands join up to fight.

Allied soldiers are rescued from France.

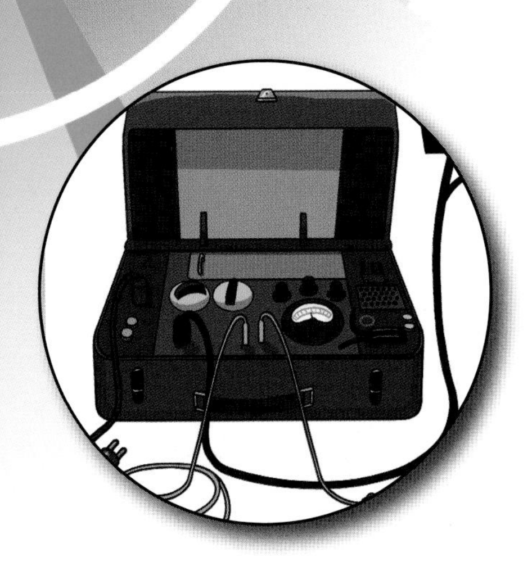

Spies find out vital information.

IT'S WAR!

Adolf Hitler was the leader of the Nazi Party in Germany. The Nazis believed German **Aryans** were the master race. They wanted Germany to be powerful. In 1933, the Nazi Party came to power and Hitler became Germany's leader.

Hitler wanted a new and powerful Germany. He wanted to get back the lands Germany had lost in World War 1. So in 1938, Hitler sent troops into Austria and Czechoslovakia.

Britain and France were alarmed. They warned Hitler that they would go to war with Germany if he invaded Poland. But Hitler took no notice of the warnings. In September 1939, he sent troops into Poland. On 3rd September, Britain and France went to war with Germany.

The Evening News

3rd September 1939

BRITAIN AND FRANCE AT WAR WITH GERMANY!

Prime Minister Neville Chamberlain announced today that Britain and France are at war with Germany. The British public have mixed feelings about the news.

Arnold Jones, 58, a shopkeeper, said: 'I think we should go to war, but I'm worried too. War will be bad for business. However, we must get rid of Hitler. If we don't, we could be next.'

Joan Mann, 29, disagreed. She said: 'My father was killed in World War One. It was terrible. I'm against war. We should try and sort things out peacefully.'

Jim Brown, 19, said: 'Hitler is a **dictator**. I read that he wants to kill Jews. We must stop him! I'm going to join up – but army life will be a big change for me.'

BRITAIN
DECLARES
AR
NEWS
THE
TRUTH

ARMY

JOINING UP

Thousands of people joined up when war broke out. They joined the army, the navy or the air force. Men were allowed to fight but women did other jobs. Most of these people had never been in the forces. They went to training camps to learn about military life.

Monday 10th July 1940:

My first day at army camp! It's very different from my old job in the butcher's shop.

First, I was given my army kit, two blankets and a kit bag. Then we had an inspection on the parade ground. The sergeant yelled at me because I wasn't standing to attention properly.

Next, we looked at the Nissen hut where we will sleep. The hut looks like a tunnel. After that, the sergeant told us about our training. We have to do cross-country runs, **assault courses** and **drills**. We have to learn survival skills. We will also have weapons training. We will learn how to take a gun apart, clean it and put it back together again – and we will learn how to fire it!

Dressed to kill

Everyone who joined up had to wear uniform. British soldiers wore a khaki uniform called battledress.

Helmet – made of steel with net over the top

Badges – show the name of the soldier's regiment

Belt – pouches hold equipment such as **ammunition**, a water bottle and a **bayonet**

Rifle with carrying strap

Deep pockets – for maps and other items

The word khaki means dust-coloured in **Urdu**.

Kit bag – holds spare clothes, army boots and washing and shaving kit

A SOLDIER IN FULL BATTLEDRESS

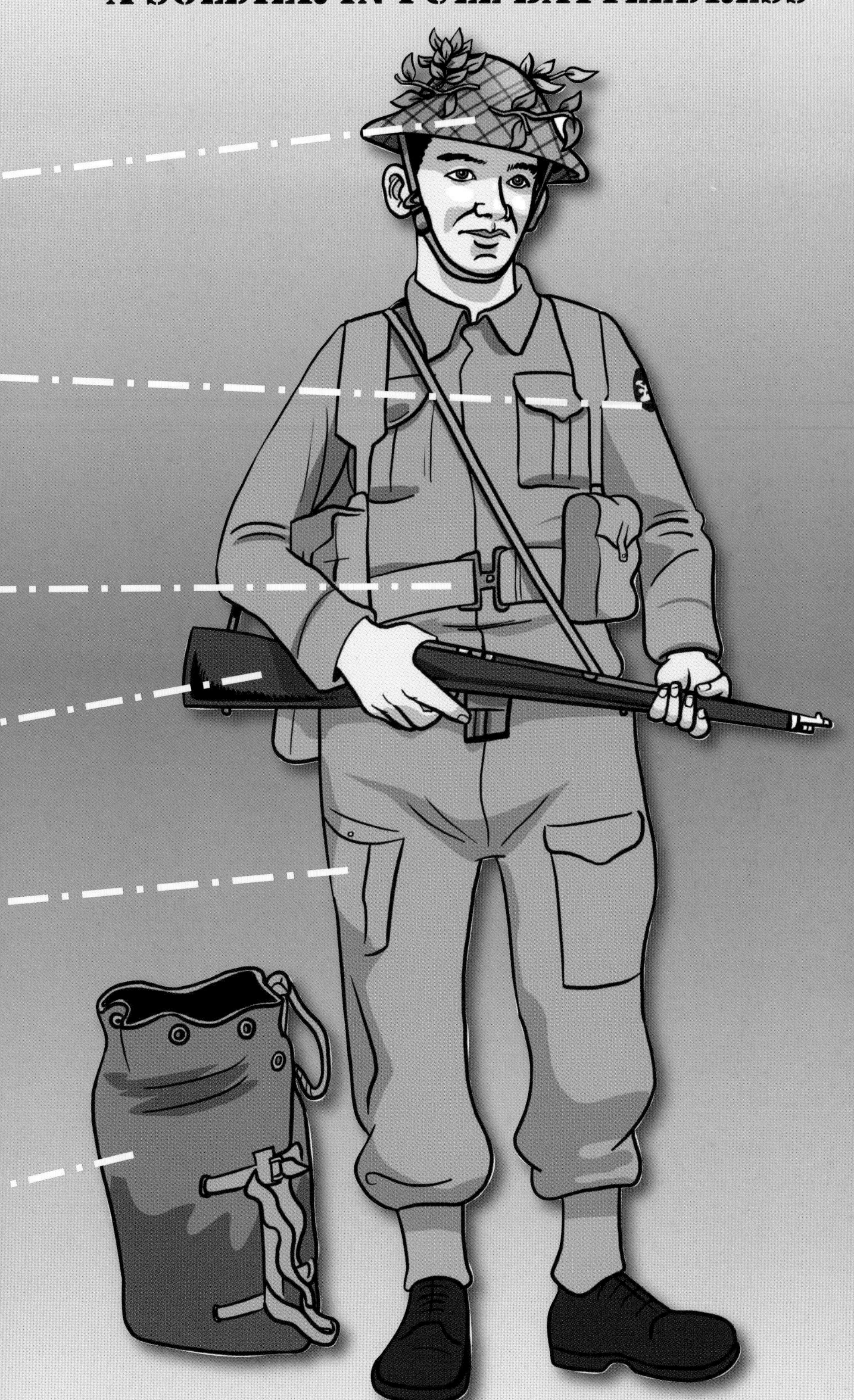

THE BIG RESCUE

In 1940, the Germans invaded France. British and French troops tried to stop them. Then they got trapped on the beaches at Dunkirk. Winston Churchill was the new British prime minister. He ordered a big sea rescue to pick up the stranded soldiers.

5, Long Road
Old Town
Essex

10th June 1940

Dear Mr Churchill,

My son, Fred, was one of the British soldiers trapped at Dunkirk in France. Today, I found out that he is safe. He told me all about the rescue.

He said that British and French soldiers were trapped on the beaches by the Germans. Then you ordered any ship, large or small, to go and pick up the stranded soldiers. Large Allied ships out at sea couldn't get close enough to the beaches. The small boats that sailed over from Britain could! The soldiers waded out to them and the boats took the soldiers to the large Allied ships.

It was a brilliant plan. Thank you!

Yours sincerely.

Joan Evans (Mrs)

The Dunkirk rescue

The Dunkirk rescue was called Operation Dynamo. More than 900 Allied ships and boats took part in it. It took place between 26th May and 4th June 1940. There were **minesweepers**, **destroyers** and lots of small boats, too. Almost 340,000 troops were rescued – but more than 40,000 vehicles had to be left behind.

OPERATION DYNAMO

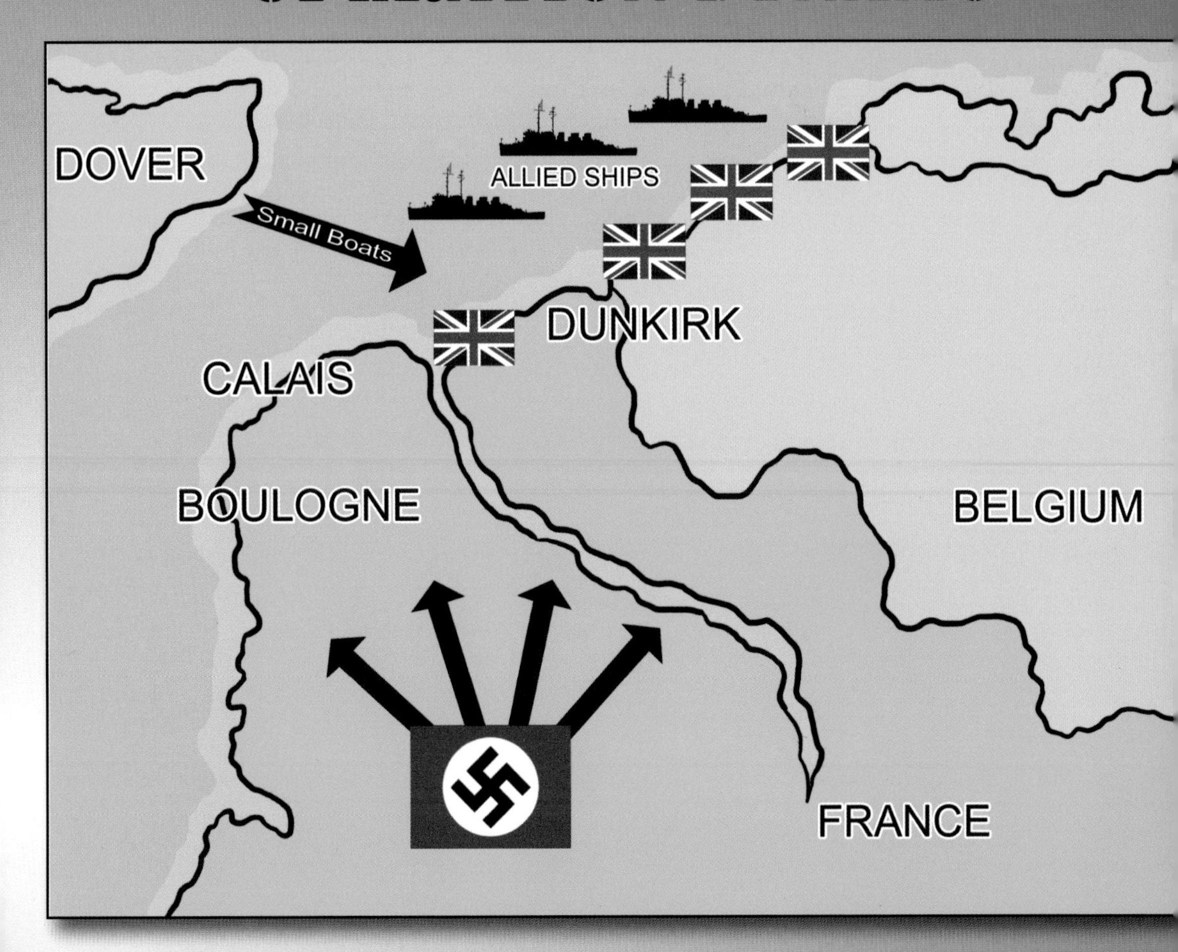

The smallest boat in the rescue was the *Tamzine*. A Belgian trawler had to tow her back to England afterwards!

CLOSE-UP: I SPY

Spies were important in the war. Both the enemy and the **Allies** had spies. The spies found out information about the enemy and sent it back to their government.

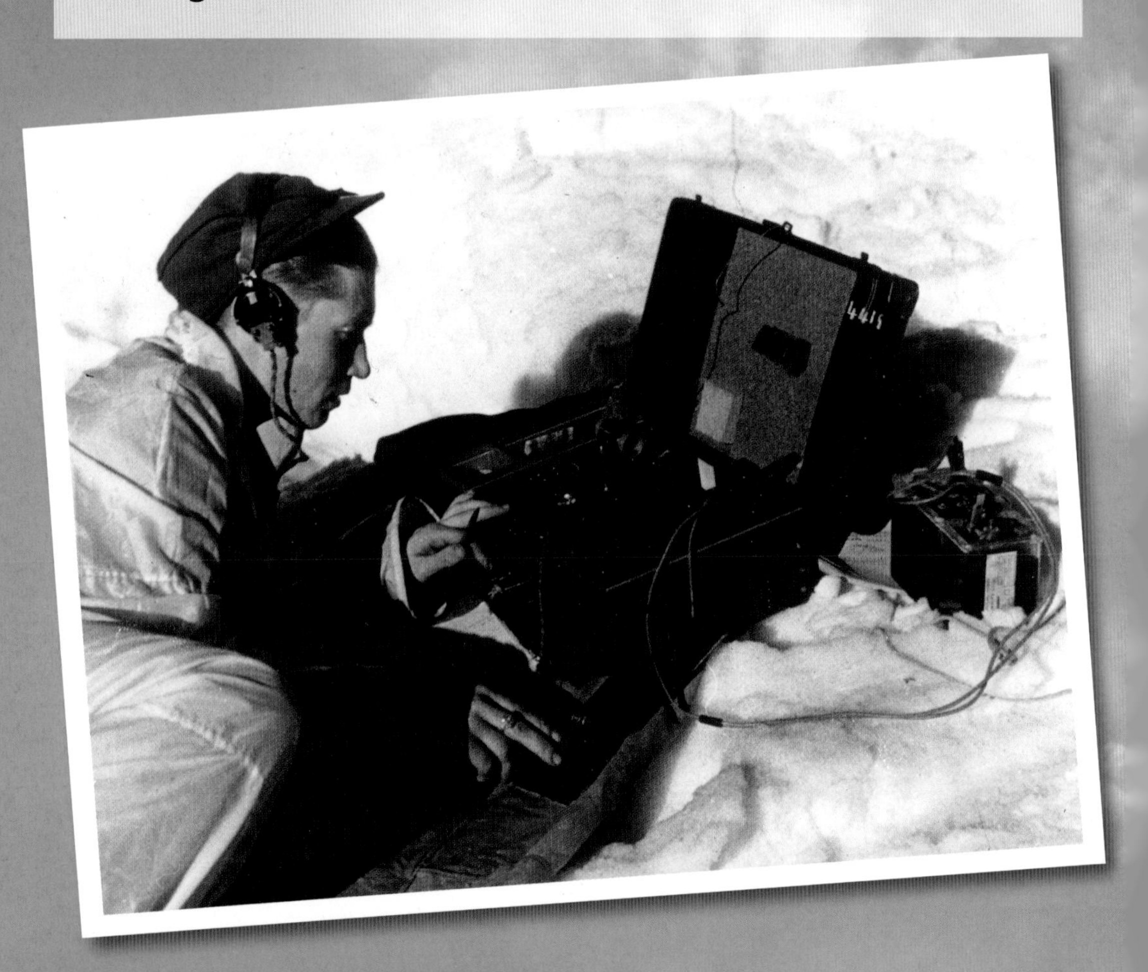

The suitcase here has a hidden radio. The spy is using it to send secret information.

This is how the suitcase worked.

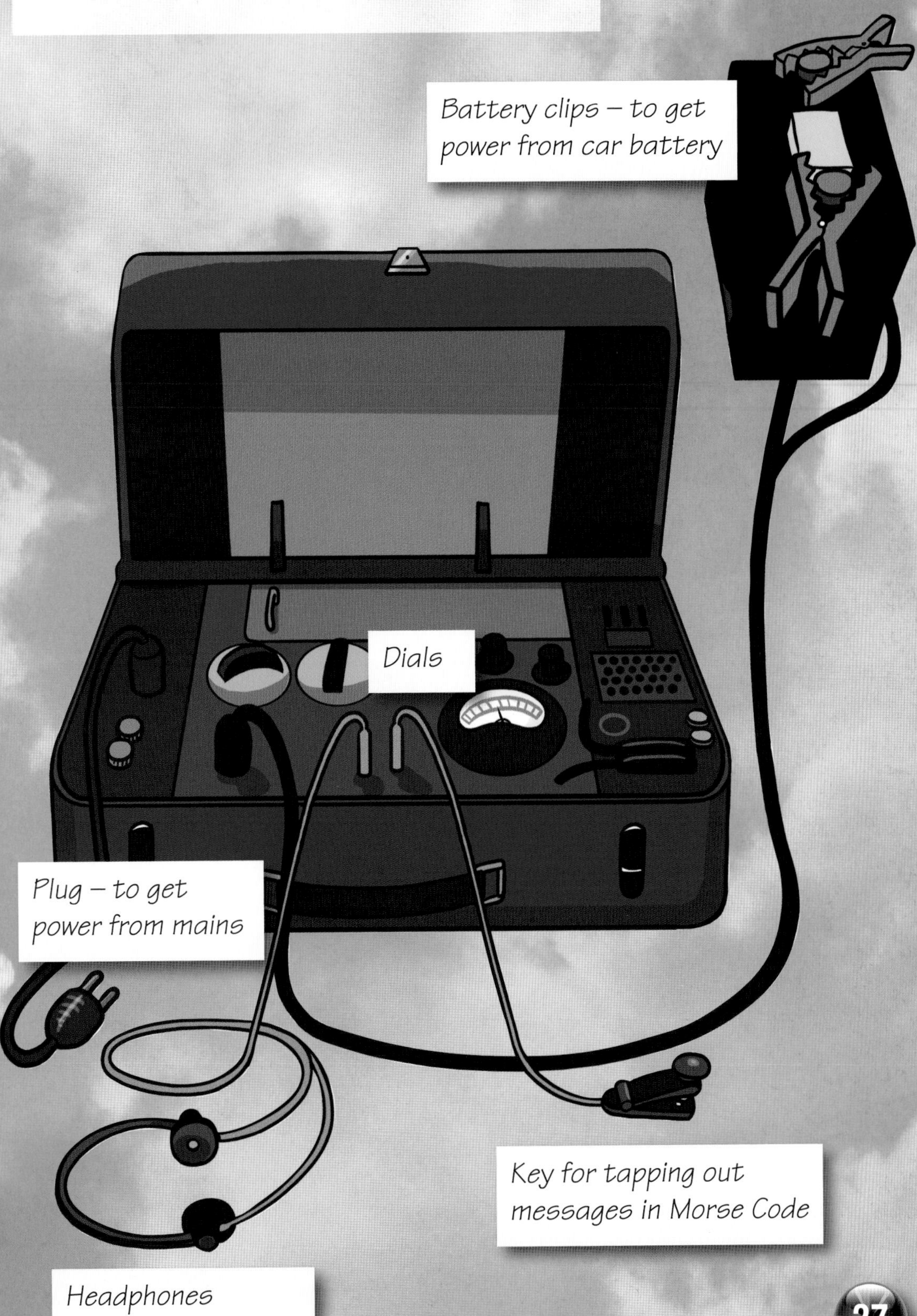

Spies used gadgets to help them get information and send it back.

Spies also used gadgets to protect themselves from the enemy.

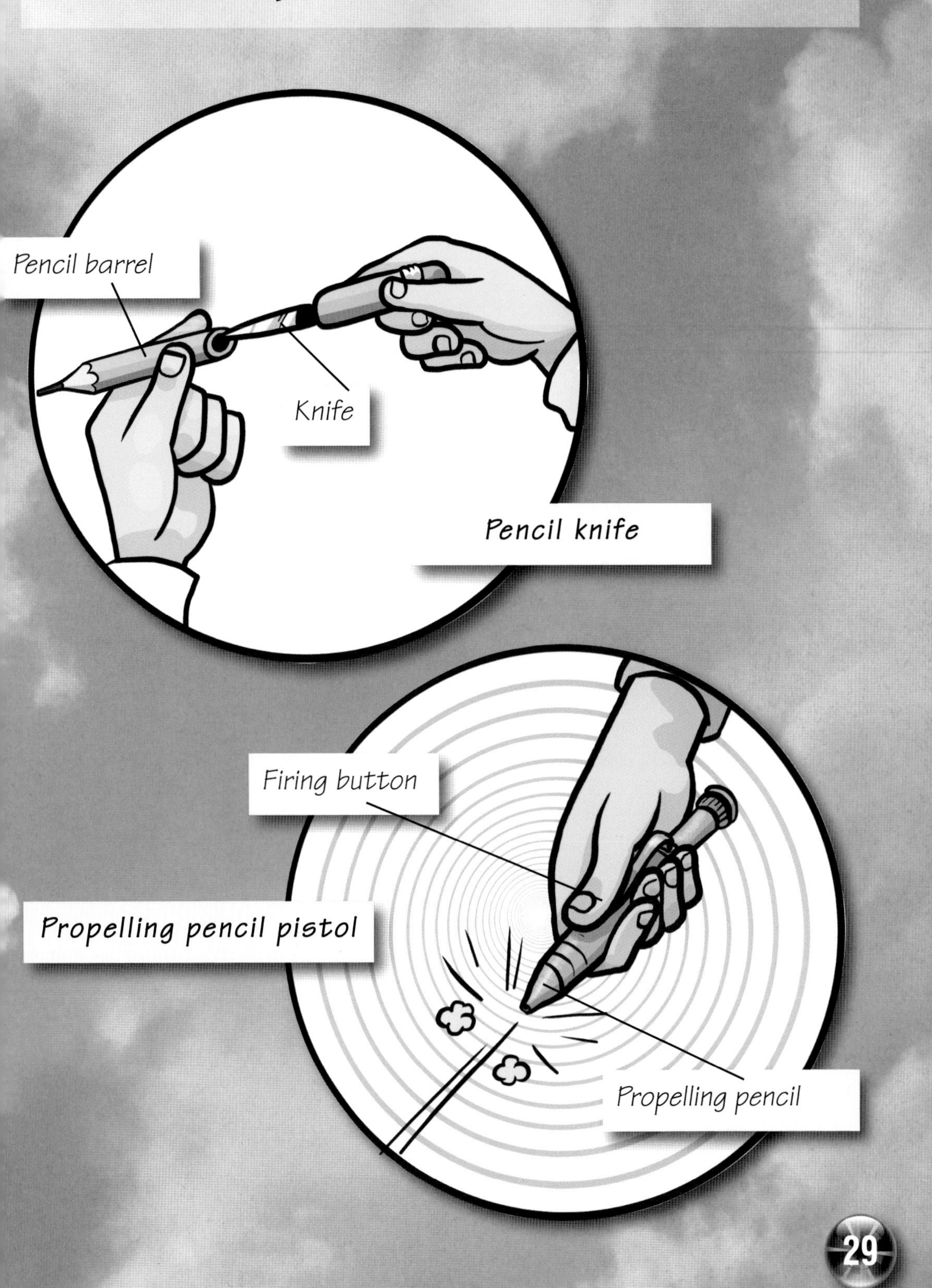

getty

FIGHTING BACK

The Germans had **occupied** France. Many French people still wanted to fight the enemy. They could only fight secretly so they set up the French Resistance. The Resistance helped Allied soldiers escape from France.

Carl

James Owen is a British airman. He was shot down last night in Calais. He hurt his leg when he landed by parachute. We must get him to a **safe house** tonight. Can Henri hide him at the farm? We must get him out of the country as soon as we can. The Germans saw a British plane crash last night. They are searching the area.

Marie

Marie

Henri will meet you both at the church at 9 pm. He will hide Owen at the farm. Pierre will get Owen out of France tomorrow. He will take him across the Channel in his fishing boat. They will leave on the dawn tide.

Carl

Resistance groups

Most occupied countries had resistance groups. These groups had to meet in secret. They used secret messages and codes. They helped Allied prisoners escape. They also made things difficult for the enemy by blowing up factories and railway lines.

Resistance groups needed weapons that were easy to hide and light to carry.

FRANCE

This knife was hidden under clothes.

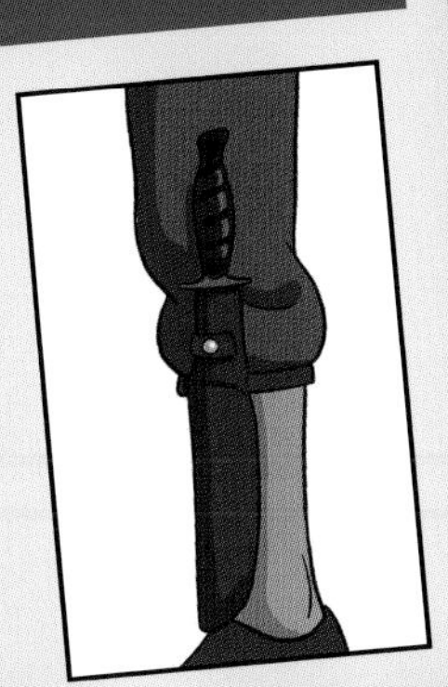

ITALY

This gun had a silencer to stop the sound of the shot.

DENMARK

This gun was light to carry and easy to use.

DOGFIGHTS

Many World War Two planes were small and only carried a pilot. Pilots learned to fight each other in close combat. These fights were called dogfights. Pilots only had ten hours of training before their first battle.

A CLOSE CALL: a play for radio

CAST:

Clark A new pilot
Denson The **Squadron** Leader

SCENE:

Clark is in his plane. He is about to fight the enemy for the first time. He's in radio contact with Denson.

CLARK: The enemy is in front of me!
DENSON: Good! Fire when you are close to him.
CLARK: Oh no! I've missed him. Where's he gone?

DENSON: Watch out! I can see him. He's coming up behind you.

CLARK: I can't see him!

DENSON (loudly): Watch out! He's going to attack you.

CLARK: What do I do?

DENSON (firmly): Dive down! I'm going after him.

SFX: Machine-gun fire

CLARK: You got him! His plane's going down!

DENSON: That was close!

CLARK: Thanks, sir! You saved my life.

Battle of Britain

In 1940, Hitler sent planes to attack Britain from the air. This air attack was called *The Battle of Britain.* It took place in the skies above the south of England. British people watched the battle from the ground.

A German Messerscmitt chasing a British Spitfire

German planes were bigger and slower than British planes. British planes were small and quick. They were better at fighting in close combat. After three months, Hitler stopped sending planes to attack Britain.

WWII FACT

The Spitfire's top speed was 582 kph!

D-DAY

On 6th June 1944, Allied forces landed in France. They took the Germans by surprise and beat them. This was D-Day. After this day, the Allies began to push the Germans back across Europe.

WWII FACT

During D-Day, planes dropped folding motorbikes into France. The Allied airmen used them when they landed.

Chapter 10

A Great Day for Churchill

Winston Churchill helped to plan the D-Day landings. They took over a year to plan. The date was kept top secret. That's why it was called 'D-Day'.

On D-Day, 156,000 British, American and Canadian troops crossed the English Channel. They landed on five beaches in Normandy. The beaches had code-names: *Omaha*, *Utah*, *Gold*, *Juno* and *Sword*. D-Day was planned down to the finest detail.

American troops land on Omaha beach.

British troops land on Sword beach.

Hitler thought the invasion was going to happen in Calais, 140 km away. The D-Day landings were a surprise to the enemy. The Allies still had to fight hard. More than 3,000 Allied troops died on D-Day itself.

The Allies won and slowly they drove the Germans back. By August, Paris was free. The end of the war in Europe was near.

VE Day

On 8th May 1945 Germany surrendered. The war was over in Europe. People celebrated **VE** day all over the world.

In New York, people tossed paper streamers out of the office windows.

In Paris, there were street parties.

In Moscow and London, there were firework displays and parades.

Crowds cheered Winston Churchill and the Royal Family outside Buckingham Palace.

GLOSSARY

Allies (Allied)	countries that joined together to fight against Germany, Italy and Japan during World War Two. The Allies included Britain, France and the USA.
Ammunition	bullets, shells and other things that can be fired
Aryans	people with white skin and fair hair
Assault course(s)	obstacles that you have to get under, over or through as part of a training exercise.
Bayonet	blade put on a rifle, to stab with
Destroyer	a small, fast warship
Dictator	ruler or leader who makes his own laws
Drill(s)	doing something over and over again to get it right
Minesweepers	a warship that looks for mines and destroys them
Occupied	the enemy has invaded the country
Resistance	secret group of people who work against the enemy
Safe house	place of shelter from the enemy
Squadron	team of planes – the leader of the team is called a squadron leader.
Urdu	a language spoken in India
VE	stands for 'Victory in Europe'

INDEX